Discerning and Defeating End Time Spirits.

E. C. Nakeli

SEKEL GOSPEL INSTITUTE
SHINING THE LIGHT OF GOD'S WORD

BETHANY HOUSE OF WORSHIP

© 2025 SEKEL Gospel Institute & Bethany House of Worship, Germany

For your questions and publishing needs, write to:

E.C. Nakeli

Karlstraße 4

75053 Gondelsheim

Germany

E-mail: ecnakeli@yahoo.com

All rights reserved. No part of this publication may be reproduced, stored in a retrieval systems, or transmitted in ay form or by any means— for example, electronic, photocopy, recording—without the prior written permission of the publisher. The only exception is brief quotations in printed reviews.

Rising Beyond Your Pain / E.C. Nakeli ISBN: 978-1-945055-20-1

Unless otherwise indicated, Scriptures references are from THE HOLY BIBLE, NEW INTERNATIONAL VERSION®, NIV® Copyright © 1973, 1978, 1984, 2011 by Biblica, Inc™ Used by permission. All rights reserved worldwide.

Table of Contents

Dedication..

Introduction..

Part 1:..

The spirit of Ephraim..

Chapter One ....

Discerning and Defeating The spirit of Ephraim-1 ....

   The desire/passion to be involved in everything..........................

      How to defeat this desire/passion to be involved in everything

   The incapacity to celebrate the success/victory of others in spite even when it benefits you..

      How to defeat this incapacity to celebrate others ....

   Deriving joy and satisfaction to have accomplished more than others...

      How to defeat the spirit of superior accomplishments 1

Chapter Two 20

Discerning and defeating the spirit of Ephraim – 2 20

   Deriving satisfaction from being better than others (Judges 8:2-3).............. 20

      Defeating the spirit of superiority 21

   The capacity to generate internal strife 22

      How to avoid strife 23

   An attitude of entitlement... 24

      Defeating the entitlement mentality 26

Chapter Three 28

Discerning and defeating the spirit of Ephraim - 3 28

      Self-exaltation 28

The inability to accept rejection without resorting to damage and destruction 29
    How to defeat this tendency to negatively react to rejection 31
The inability to repent 32
    How to defeat this unrepentant spirit 33
    34
        defeat the spirit of envy 35
        our 37
        nd defeating the spirit of Ephraim – 4 37
        dultery 37
        defeat this spirit of adultery 38
        o the world for remedy 38
        o defeat the tendency to look for alternatives 40
        od and deceit 40
    ow to defeat the spirit of falsehood and deceit 41
    Compromise and complacency 42
        How to defeat compromise and complacency 42
    Self-deception 44
        How to defeat self-deception 45
    Hidden sins 45
        Defeating the tendency to hide one's own sins 45

Chapter five 47
Deliverance from the spirit of Ephraim 47

Part 2: 51
The spirit of gehazi 51

Chapter six 53
Discerning and defeating the Spirit of Gehazi 53

- Judging by external appearances 53
  - *How to overcome this tendency to focus on the external* 55
  - Spiritual disconnect 56
    - *How to overcome spiritual disconnect* 58

Chapter Seven 61
Discerning and defeating the spirit of Gehazi – 2 61
- Covetousness 61
  - Manifestations of covetousness 63
    - *How to defeat covetousness* 66
  - Spiritual "parasiting" 67

Chapter Eight 71
Deliverance from the spirit of Gehazi 71

Part 3: 73
The spirit of Jezebel 73

Chapter Nine 75
Discerning and defeating the spirit of Jezebel 75
- How the spirit manifests 76
  - *How to defeat the afore listed manifestation of the spirit of jezebel* 80

Chapter Ten 83
Discerning and defeating the spirit of Jezebel - 2 83
- Further manifestations of the spirit of jezebel 83
  - *How to overcome the spirit of jezebel* 86

Chapter eleven 89
Deliverance from the spirit of Jezebel 89

Part 4: 93
The spirit of Judas Iscariot 93

Chapter Twelve ... 95
Discerning and defeating the spirit of Judas Iscariot – 1 ... 95
- Where it will manifest ... 96

Chapter Thirteen ... 101
Reasons why people will betray each other ... 101

Chapter Fourteen ... 107
How to defeat the spirit of Judas Iscariot – 1 ... 107

Chapter Fifteen ... 113
How to defeat the spirit of Judas Iscariot – 2 ... 113

Chapter Sixteen ... 123
Deliverance from the spirit of betrayal ... 123
Conclusion ... 126

Dedication

To all those currently enrolled in God's end times army, to all future enrollees into God's army; all those through whom El-Gibor, the Lord strong and mighty, is raising a standard against the enemy advance.

Introduction

There are several spirits being released by the enemy into society at large and the church in particular.

Some of these spirits are very obvious and can easily be identified while others are more subtle and can operate in the lives of even the most anointed of God's servants without them detecting its presence.

In this series, "Discerning and Defeating the End time Spirits" we will begin exposing these spirits, beginning with the very subtle ones and moving on the obvious ones.

In Volume 1, we will see how they operate and how you can identify if they operate in your live and provide steps to deliverance. In subsequent volumes we shall continue to examine other spirits which will be rampant in these last days. We examine spirits that seek to control individuals, entire lineages, communities and even people groups.

Part 1: The spirit of Ephraim

Chapter One

Discerning and Defeating The spirit of Ephraim-1

The name Ephraim is first mentioned in the Bible as the second born son of Joseph in Egypt. It was used to designate one of the tribes of Israel and later it was figuratively used to refer to the northern kingdom of Israel as opposed to the southern kingdom of Judah.

Ephraim means "ash heap" or "twice fruitful". Ephraim was destined for greatness; he was prophetically ordained to be greater than his brother even though he was the second son of Joseph (Genesis 48:20). Ephraim was a leader of one of the four camps made up of three tribes each during the Exodos (Numbers 2:24). He was destined to fly with the stars, so to speak. He was to be a role model and reference of one blessed by the God of Israel, as it was to be said, ""In your name will Israel pronounce this blessing: "May God make you like Ephraim..." (Genesis 48:20).

The spirit of Ephraim is the spirit that operates in many a very fruitful, talented, and gifted person. It usually seeks to take hold of the lives of those on whom is a prophetic word, those called to lead amongst

God's people. Those called to fly high and ride the trails of excellence. It is more dangerous than other end-time spirits because it operates primarily in the lives of those called to lead.

Many people celebrate this dangerous spirit without knowing, because it is associated with greatness, excellence, and leadership. Like every good thing God created on this side of eternity the enemy seeks, and seems to succeed, to contaminate and pervert. In the sections that follow, we will discern this spirit of Ephraim and see how we can defeat this spirit in the lives of individuals and the church.

What are the manifestations of the spirit of Ephraim and how can we defeat this spirit?

The desire/passion to be involved in everything

"Now the Ephraimites asked Gideon, "Why have you treated us like this? Why didn't you call us when you went to fight Midian?" And they challenged him vigorously" (Judges 8:1)

Israel had backslidden and came under immense oppression from the Midianites. The whole nation was suffering and the Lord decided to bring about deliverance as an answer to the outcry of the Israelites. As is always His way, He chose an obscure, fearful Gideon to use for this task. Despite the difficulties, the Lord wrought a great victory through the hand of Gideon. It was cause for the whole Israel to celebrate because someone had brought them freedom from under the oppressive hand of Midian. But because Ephraim was not consulted, he was ready to start an internal strife instead of being part of the celebration.

People ruled by the spirit of Ephraim do not celebrate the victories and successes of others despite them. They want to be involved in everything and feel disrespected or left out if they are not consulted or brought in to participate. This leads us to our next manifestation of this spirit.

How to defeat this desire/passion to be involved in everything

1. Understand that you are just a part of the body

You are just a tiny little part of the body and have not been equipped to do everything and be involved in everything. It is written that, "From him the whole body, joined and held together by every supporting ligament, grows and builds itself up in love, as each part does its work" (Ephesians 4:16). Not as one part does everything but as each part does its role. How would it be if the eye decided that it wanted to be involved in tasting the food you ate?

2. Deliberately delegate power and fully trust your delegates until otherwise

Mistrust in others, which often arises out of personal insecurities, is often the root cause of someone trying to do everything and be involved in everything. One way to defeat this monster is to go against the fear of trusting and entrusting others with important tasks. In other words, do not always wait for trust to be earned. Sometimes, you have to first lend your trust.

3. Deliberately leave some things undone

What I mean is, sometimes you need to withhold yourself from doing the things you are well capable of doing. Paul said, he refrained from baptizing people, except one or two households in the early days of his ministry. In this way his coworkers were involved in carrying baptizing the thousands he led to the Lord.

The incapacity to celebrate the success/victory of others despite you, even when it benefits you

> "The Ephraimite forces were called out, and they crossed over to Zaphon. They said to Jephthah, "Why did you go to fight the Ammonites without calling us to go with you? We're going to burn down your house over your head" (Judges 12:1).

The Bible says, like in the previous case above, all of Israel including Ephraim was in distress because of the Ammonite oppression (Judges 10:9), when God raised up Jephthah, and wrought a great victory that brought about freedom to all Israel, even at the cost of the life of his daughter, Ephraim would not celebrate the victory because they were not involved. They were not happy that someone else would receive the praise and be celebrated. They were not happy that they weren't at the center of the victory and decided to stir up trouble.

People with the spirit of Ephraim are not happy when people succeed without them, they would rather destroy the success than celebrate with them or celebrate them. They are quick to find fault even if it means manufacturing one themselves just to denigrate the other.

Do you celebrate the victories, successes, and triumphs of others even when they ignore you? Is there a spirit of competitiveness that motivates your pursuits in life? Do you measure yourself and accomplishments with others? This leads us to our next manifestation: deriving joy and satisfaction from having accomplished more than others. But. Let us first see how we can defeat this manifestation of the incapacity to celebrate others.

How to defeat this incapacity to celebrate others
1. Consciously offer thanks to God for the victory and successes of others.

One of the things that bring joy to the human heart is the practice of thanksgiving. As you thank God for something, your heart is spiritually drawn to identify with and rejoice over, and with the thing in question.

2. Deliberately congratulate people on their success

As you deliberately congratulate people on their victories and success, even if your heart doesn't mean it at first, by the second or third time you take the initiative to celebrate someone, the resistance offered by the fallen nature in you will be broken.

3. Widen your perspective

The root cause of this malady of the inability to celebrate others is a narrow perspective on life that narrows one's vision through the eyes of self. When you expand your horizon and broaden your perspective to view things through the lens of the kingdom, you come to understand that the success and victory of one is the success and victory of the Kingdom of God. You rise above pettiness to be kingdom minded.

Deriving joy and satisfaction to have accomplished more than others

"But he answered them, "What have I accomplished compared to you? Aren't the gleanings of Ephraim's grapes better than the full grape harvest of Abiezer? 3 God gave Oreb and Zeeb, the Midianite leaders, into your hands. What was I able to do compared to you?" At this, their resentment against him subsided" (Judges 8:2-3).

Ephraim became resentful because they weren't involved in this battle by the one the Lord had chosen to work with. They were used to glorying in success, in leading, in having people rally in their land and from there lunch the war (see Judges 3:27, and 4:5). However, in this case the rallying cry came from another land and Ephraim was not pleased with that. Now, they became angry and resentful when God decided to use someone else without consulting them.

Never come to the point where you begin to oppose what God is doing through another person because it did not branch out from you, or because you were not consulted.

This spirit is one of the reasons of the strife and competition in the Body of Christ today. Ministries and denominations trying to outspend each other, outshine each other. All of this is cloaked in religious language called vision. Pastors and Apostles are not satisfied till they have outclassed everybody else and become the talk of their locality, nation, and world.

Nothing appeases the spirit of Ephraim than the feeling of accomplishing more than others have or would. When Gideon pointed out the greater accomplishments of Ephraim, they were pleased and satisfied. They were not pleased with the victory over the enemy, which was for the benefit of the whole nation, but were pleased to be reminded of their own greatness. It is very similar to the next point.

How to defeat the spirit of superior accomplishments
1. Depend on the Lord for everything

When we use human strength and abilities to serve, we tend to glory in self. That is why Peter admonished that "If anyone speaks, they should do so as one who speaks the very words of God. If anyone serves, they should do so with the strength God provides, so that in all things God may be praised through Jesus Christ. To him be the glory and the power for ever and ever. Amen" (1Peter 4:11).

2. Understand that it is God who works through you

When you see everything you are able to do as an extension of the work of the Almighty through you, there will be no room to derive any satisfaction from a sense of superior accomplishments. The prophet Isaiah said, "Lord, you establish peace for us; all that we have accomplished you have done for us" (Isaiah 26:12) and Paul declared that, "^{13} for it is God who works in you to will and to act in order to fulfill his good purpose" (Philippians 2:13). Why will you take glory for what Another does through you, knowing He can use anything?

3. Deliberately return all glory to God for any success or accomplishments

The Psalmist prayed, "Not to us, Lord, not to us but to your name be the glory, because of your love and faithfulness" (Psalm 115:1). To overcome this temptation to glory in yourself and take pride in what you have accomplished as compared to others, learn to declare like the Psalmist above each time you succeed in doing something.

Chapter Two

Discerning and defeating the spirit of Ephraim – 2

Deriving satisfaction from being better than others (Judges 8:2-3)

Very similar to the deriving satisfaction from having accomplished more than others, is deriving satisfaction from being better than others. This can be manifested in appearance, in possession, in resources,

- Better dressed
- Better living
- Better cars
- Better church building

For people operating under this spirit of Ephraim, the motivation of all they do, the sacrifices they make, the investments they make all derive from this "better than thou" attitude. This motivation may sometimes be cloaked in a spiritual language, but the Spirit of God cannot be deceived. Ephraim was appeased when they heard that the produce of their land was better than that from where Gideon came. This spirit is what pushes racism, tribalism, and other forms of nepotism.

The many exclusive clubs, sometimes disguised as ministerial alliances in the church, or partnership circles are likely offspring from this spirit of being better than others. Think of churches or ministries that will not associate with other churches or ministries, are they motivated by the Spirit of Christ? This spirit of superiority can lead to internal strife, which brings us to the next manifestation.

Defeating the spirit of superiority
1. Self- abasement and self-effacement

One thing that kept David from glorying in himself was his capacity to self-abase and self-efface. He took a conscious decision to humiliate himself. He told the daughter of Saul, "I will become even more undignified than this, and I will be humiliated in my own eyes. But by these slave girls you spoke of, I will be held in honor" (2 Samuel 6:22). He allowed himself to be disrespected on several occasions and refused to defend himself.

2. Acknowledge the gift and working of grace

"For I am the least of the apostles and do not even deserve to be called an apostle, because I persecuted the church of God. 10 But by the grace of God I am what I am, and his grace to me was not without effect. No, I worked harder than all of them—yet not I, but the grace of God that was with me" (1 Corinthians 15:9-10).

"I became a servant of this gospel by the gift of God's grace given me through the working of his power. 8 Although I am less than the least of all the Lord's people, this grace was given me:

to preach to the Gentiles the boundless riches of Christ" (Ephesians 3:7-8)

"For who makes you different from anyone else? What do you have that you did not receive? And if you did receive it, why do you boast as though you did not?" (1 Corinthians 4:7).

In the above verses, we see the great apostle Paul self-abasing and acknowledging the gift and working of grace in his life and through him. That is how he defeated the spirit of superiority, and that is how you too, can defeat it.

The capacity to generate internal strife

"Jephthah answered, "I and my people were engaged in a great struggle with the Ammonites, and although I called, you didn't save me out of their hands. ³ When I saw that you wouldn't help, I took my life in my hands and crossed over to fight the Ammonites, and the Lord gave me the victory over them. Now why have you come up today to fight me?"⁴ Jephthah then called together the men of Gilead and fought against Ephraim. The Gileadites struck them down because the Ephraimites had said, "You Gileadites are renegades from Ephraim and Manasseh" (Judges 12:2-4).

Even though Ephraim came very confrontational, ready to stir up trouble, Jephthah responded in a way that would appease the Ephraimites. But they stirred up more trouble by insulting the Gileadites. This spirit is ready to pick on very minor differences and use them to generate strife amongst brethren.

They called them renegades just to stir up internal strife. But this time they met their match. Jephthah was not going to make them feel good about themselves like Gideon did. Remember, it was Israel who came seeking for Jephthah when they were in distress. If Ephraim was so qualified, why did they not seek his help to lead the battle against the Ammonites? This arrogant and self-exalting attitude is the reason 42,000 lives were lost.

Personal ego can be very costly, and the body of Christ has suffered untold damages because of the personal ego of some. Just think of it, how many souls are heading to the lake of fire because of internal strife within ministries and between ministries? This leads us to the next manifestation, but before then let us see how we can avoid unnecessary strife

How to avoid strife
1. Crucify all selfish ambition

One thing that pushes strife amongst people is selfish ambition. If you would crucify selfish ambition, it would greatly diminish your capacity to initiate internal strife, and enhance your capacity to resist strife. Paul exhorts us to "[3] Do nothing out of selfish ambition or vain conceit. Rather, in humility value others above yourselves, [4] not looking to your own interests but each of you to the interests of the others (Philippians 2:3-4).

Ask yourself each time, "what is motivating this action of mine?" if your sincere response to that question has anything to do with selfish ambition, then do not do it.

2. Crucify the lusts of life

The lusts of the heart is another source of strife among people. James admonished the saints in this regard: "What causes fights and quarrels among you? Don't they come from your desires that battle within you? 2 You desire but do not have, so you kill. You covet but you cannot get what you want, so you quarrel and fight. You do not have because you do not ask God" (James 4:1-2).

> ### An attitude of entitlement
> "The people of Joseph said to Joshua, "Why have you given us only one allotment and one portion for an inheritance? We are a numerous people, and the Lord has blessed us abundantly." [15] "If you are so numerous," Joshua answered, "and if the hill country of Ephraim is too small for you, go up into the forest and clear land for yourselves there in the land of the Perizzites and Rephaites. [16] The people of Joseph replied, "The hill country is not enough for us, and all the Canaanites who live in the plain have chariots fitted with iron, both those in Beth Shan and its settlements and those in the Valley of Jezreel. [17] But Joshua said to the tribes of Joseph—to Ephraim and Manasseh—"You are numerous and very powerful. You will have not only one allotment [18] but the forested hill country as well. Clear it, and its farthest limits will be yours; though the Canaanites have chariots fitted with iron and though they are strong, you can drive them out." (Joshua 17:14-17)

By the direction of God through Moses, and by casting of lots, the tribes had received their inheritance. However, Ephraim thought what they were given was too small. They said because they were a great people they needed more than had been allotted them.

People with the spirit of Ephraim have this tendency to think they are entitled:

- Entitled to be heard
- Entitled to the pulpit
- Entitled to be called into leadership
- Entitled to be ordained
- Entitled to be recognized and celebrated
- Entitled to more than they have received or are receiving

This is the tendency that leads to rebellion, betrayal, and schism within churches.

People are willing to scatter a church or ministry just because they feel they are getting less than they were entitled to. We will see this tendency increasingly manifest even in homes. Children will increasingly feel they are entitled to certain privileges and will be ready to destroy anything or anyone to satisfy their sense of entitlement. Employees will become increasingly entitled to things or benefits. Civil servants will increasingly become civil masters because of the sense of entitlement.

In the case of Ephraim, Joshua's response to them couldn't have been better. Great people do not have a sense of entitlement, they are willing and ready to chart out new territories for themselves. They do not fight over what others have worked for. If you think you are so gifted and need more ministry opportunities, you do not need to split the church to start yours, you can peacefully leave and chart out a new territory.

Do not kill your parents because you feel entitled. Do not destroy that business started by another because you feel entitled. Chart your own course. Conquer your own territory. Ephraim described themselves as a numerous and powerful people, yet they were afraid to go confront the Canaanites and extend their territory. Why would you destroy what others have sweated for? Why should others be deprived of their inheritance to satisfy your discontent?

Defeating the entitlement mentality
1. Understand that no man owes you anything

Entitlement mentality is a trap of hell to keep you angry, disappointed, and disillusioned. All good gifts come from God and not man or the systems put in place by man. It is written, "Every good and perfect gift is from above, coming down from the Father of the heavenly lights, who does not change like shifting shadows" (James 1:17).

2. Shift your focus from man and systems to God

When you look to man or to systems as your source, your life will be full of disappointments. Truly, no human being or system owes you anything. John the Baptist said, "a person can receive only what is given them from heaven" (John 3:27). In other words, receive from heaven and no one can stop it or change it.

David said, "I lift up my eyes to the mountains— where does my help come from? 2 My help comes from the Lord, the Maker of heaven and earth" (Psalm 121:1-2). Your help is not from the hills and mountains of human society. Your help comes from the Lord who made heaven and earth. Once during a famine in the land of Israel caused by an enemy blockade, a woman called out to the king for help, and his response was, ""If the Lord does not help you, where can I get help for you?" (2 Kings 6:27). True help originates from heaven. It is true that heaven may choose to use an individual or a system, often individuals and systems from which you have not expected anything.

Chapter Three

Discerning and defeating the spirit of Ephraim - 3
Self-exaltation

"When Ephraim spoke, people trembled; he was exalted in Israel" (Hosea 13:1a)

The spirit of Ephraim is also a spirit of self-exaltation. Ephraim, had exalted himself in Israel to the point that the rest of the nation trembled when he spoke. He had become like a father in the nation. People with the spirit of Ephraim exalt themselves over others. They want to "father" or mentor everyone else, yet they themselves are not under any clear authority. They want to be respected and to be given the last word.

They exalt themselves through religious schemes. We see this spirit rampant in the church today in the creation of titles and offices that are not even Biblical, just because people want to be exalted above others. The spirit of Ephraim makes you think that your voice has become the voice of God, and whatever you say must be accepted at face value.

The spirit of Ephraim expects and tries to cause everybody to have the same perspective as yours and those who dare to differ are crushed or driven out. The spirit of Ephraim demands conformity and promotes hypocrisy and false humility. It operates through fear, manipulation, and control. Because those who exalt themselves over others tend to use these demonic tools of control, fear, manipulation, and intimidation to bring conformity. People under its influence lack the capacity to handle rejection.

The inability to accept rejection without resorting to damage and destruction
(2 Chronicles 25:6-13)

One mark of true greatness is the ability to accept rejection without becoming retaliative. However, the spirit of Ephraim is a spirit which makes people to become vengeful and vindictive when they are rejected for one reason or another. Because the spirit of Ephraim wants to be at the center of everything, wants to be consulted, wants to be involved, and exalts itself above others, rejection is something it cannot accept.

Ephraim had been hired to fight alongside Judah against the enemy forces, at the time when the nation of Israel had become two separate nations, Israel and Judah. Through a prophecy, King Amaziah was asked to not allow the Ephraimites accompany him into battle because that would spell defeat, since Ephraim was a backslidden, idolatrous nation at the time. In obedience to the word of the Lord, the Bible says,

> "So Amaziah dismissed the troops who had come to him from Ephraim and sent them home. They were furious with Judah and left for home in a great rage… Meanwhile the troops that Amaziah had sent back and had not allowed to take part in the war raided towns belonging to Judah from Samaria to Beth Horon. They killed three thousand people and carried off great quantities of plunder" (2 Chronicles 25:10,13).

One would think that Ephraim would have gone home quietly after they were asked to. In fact, they should have rejoiced for being paid to do nothing. They could have been happy that they made such large amounts of money without putting up a fight. But the Bible say they left in fury and a great rage and resorted to raiding of towns and killing of 3000 innocent people. They were unable to deal with rejection.

In these end-times, we will increasingly see such manifestation. People rejected in love will seek the demise of the one they claimed to have loved. People rejected from leadership will try to destroy the organization they claimed to be part of.

Can you accept rejection without resorting to destroy or inflict damage on those who rejected you?

Are you scheming to destroy that business,

that ministry,

that reputation,

that marriage,

that home because you've been rejected?

Because your services were not needed?

How to defeat this tendency to negatively react to rejection
In addition to the points discussed under defeating the entitlement mentality. The following will help you guard against this tendency to violently react to rejection:

1. See rejection as a pathway to greatness

Look at people God used extraordinarily, both in Bible times and in recent history. Most of them were "victims" of rejection. However, they refused to react negatively. Moses faced rejection by his own very people, but God still used him to deliver them. David was rejected even by his brothers, but he still became king. What about Joseph?

2. Follow the example of Christ

The Lord Jesus Christ was rejected by the world He created and came to save. He would have gone back to heaven and left humanity to perish in its sin, but he lovingly served and died for humanity. He did not destroy the world for rejecting Him. He still loves the world and intercedes on her behalf.

The inability to repent

"The Lord has sent a message against Jacob; it will fall on Israel. [9] All the people will know it— Ephraim and the inhabitants of Samaria—who say with pride and arrogance of heart, [10] "The bricks have fallen down, but we will rebuild with dressed stone; the fig trees have been felled, but we will replace them with cedars." [11] But the Lord has strengthened Rezin's foes against them and has spurred their enemies on. [12] Arameans from the east and Philistines from the west have devoured Israel with open mouth. Yet for all this, his anger is not turned away, his hand is still upraised. [13] But the people have not returned to him who struck them, nor have they sought the Lord Almighty" (Isaiah 9:8-13).

The spirit of Ephraim makes people obstinate in their own ways. They refuse to respond to the word of God. They are hardened when disciplined. The spirit of Ephraim is the spirit of pride, that would rather lose everything than humble itself in repentance when rebuked or chastised. People will become increasingly unruly and hate all forms of discipline. They will rather stop serving than accept rebuke. They would rather isolate themselves than stay in the protection of a local church because of the inability to accept correction.

This inability to repent will also be directed toward man. People will find it difficult to say "I am sorry, please forgive me". Humanity will become so arrogant that people will rather destroy their homes, churches, business than apologize to their spouse, children, partners, and other stakeholders.

When is the last time you apologized to someone less powerful or less privileged with respect to the things of this life than you are? How low can you go to save your marriage, business, partnership, ministry etc.?

How to defeat this unrepentant spirit
1. Receive a new heart of flesh

Stiff-neckedness is something that is intertwined in the fallen human nature, and sometimes, even after regeneration, one has to consciously get rid of the heart of stone and receive a new heart of flesh from the Lord. He promised the children of Israel saying,

> "I will sprinkle clean water on you, and you will be clean; I will cleanse you from all your impurities and from all your idols. ^{26} I will give you a new heart and put a new spirit in you; I will remove from you your heart of stone and give you a heart of flesh. ^{27} And I will put my Spirit in you and move you to follow my decrees and be careful to keep my laws" (Ezekiel 36:25-27).

I believe the promise still stands for you and I. The heart of flesh makes it easy to repent.

2. Be quick to acknowledge guilt and ask for forgiveness

The human tendency to self-defend or self-justify is another manifestation of the spirit of Ephraim. Each action of self-justification instead of owning up and asking for forgiveness helps fortify the stronghold of the inability to repent. To weaken this stronghold, you have to do the opposite, each time you find yourself needing to defend or justify your words or actions.

Envy

"The envy also of Ephraim shall depart, and the adversaries of Judah shall be cut off: Ephraim shall not envy Judah, and Judah shall not vex Ephraim" (Isaiah 11:13).

The spirit of Ephraim is also the spirit of envy. Increasingly, people will be motivated by their quest to own what others own and occupy others' position. The world is promoting discontent among the populace and one can say, shamefully, this unbridled emotion is being promoted even in the church under the guise of prosperity.

Through the gates of covetousness people are increasingly opening up their lives to this spirit of envy. Before long they become victims of this viscous monster. It is written that, "^{14} But if you harbor bitter envy and selfish ambition in your hearts, do not boast about it or deny the truth. ^{15} Such "wisdom" does not come down from heaven but is earthly, unspiritual, demonic. ^{16} For where you have envy and selfish ambition, there you find disorder and every evil practice" (James 3:14-16).

Increasingly, this discontent that breeds disorder will lead to anarchy. People will become more brazen in taking what rightfully belongs to others so as to satisfy their lusts. In fact, we are already witnessing this in some circles where smash-and-grab is no longer punishable. This is not by accident. The social engineers in alliance with the devil have programmed communities to become entitled to things, to crave for more things, and then they diminish the means of acquiring such things, Finally, through demonic laws disguised as social justice, they make people powerless to defend themselves, thereby emboldening the less privilege to attack individuals and business so they may own what they can otherwise not possess.

How to defeat the spirit of envy

Discontent is the breeding ground of envy. Discontent itself is bred by comparing oneself with others. When you compare your status and what you possess with that of others, it makes you want to exert yourself after vanity. This exertion after vanity often leads to frustration, disappointment, and even anger, because there will always be someone who is better placed than you. How does one "kill" this spirit of envy? I believe the answer lies in contentment. Contentment is borne from gratitude for what you are and have, and a willingness to share with the less privileged.

John the Baptist told his hearers, "Be content with your pay" (Luke 3:14). The Lord Jesus told His disciples, "Watch out! Be on your guard against all kinds of greed; life does not consist in an abundance of possessions." (Luke 12:15). Paul said, "But if we have food and clothing, we will be content with that" (1 Timothy 6:8). The writer of Hebrews said, "Keep your lives free from the love of money and be content with what you have, because God has said, "Never will I leave you; never will I forsake you" (Hebrews 13:5). Contentment is the key to defeating the spirit of envy and greed. Speaking of himself, Paul said,

"[12] I know what it is to be in need, and I know what it is to have plenty. I have learned the secret of being content in any and every situation, whether well fed or hungry, whether living in plenty or in want. [13] I can do all this through him who gives me strength" (Philippians 4:13).

Chapter Four

Discerning and defeating the spirit of Ephraim – 4

Spiritual Adultery

"Ephraim is joined to idols; leave him alone! 18 Even when their drinks are gone, they continue their prostitution; their rulers dearly love shameful ways" (Hosea 4:17-18).

"I know all about Ephraim; Israel is not hidden from me. Ephraim, you have now turned to prostitution; Israel is corrupt. 4 "Their deeds do not permit them to return to their God. A spirit of prostitution is in their heart; they do not acknowledge the Lord" (Hosea 5:3-4).

The spirit of Ephraim is the spirit of both physical and spiritual adultery. People in the church will increasingly prostitute themselves with strange gods: the gods of vanity, money, beauty, sex, fame, and power. There will be an increasing number of people who appear to be on the Lord's side but who constantly eat from the table of the enemy.

Like in the days of the replacement, "they worshiped the Lord, but they also served their own gods in accordance with the customs of the nations from which they had been brought" (2 Kings 17:33). Because people are not being taught to terminate with their past, people will come into the churches but will bring with them their heathen practices tied to the demonic traditions of their ancestors. There is a mixture that is coming unless the church rises and returns to her foundations.

Because of this spiritual adultery, people will embrace physical promiscuity in order the worship their god of materialism and vanity. Think of how nation states are changing laws to make room for "sex workers". The most sacred things of the human anatomy are being used for money-making.

Adultery and fornication seem to increasingly be tolerated among the saints. This is an end time spirit. There are so called men of God with multiple sex partners. Sexual purity is becoming something exceptional instead of normal in the church.

How to defeat this spirit of adultery

The one way to defeat this spirit of spiritual adultery is to overthrow and destroy every idol in your heart and life. what are the things that are competing with your devotion to God? What are the things distracting you from the pursuit of the high calling of God on your life? You may want to write them down, pray through the list and denounce, overthrow them from your heart, and if need be destroy the ones that can be physically or mentally destroyed.

Looking to the world for remedy

"When Ephraim saw his sickness, and Judah his sores, then Ephraim turned to Assyria, and sent to the great king for help.

But he is not able to cure you, not able to heal your sores" (Hosea 5:13).

""Ephraim is like a dove, easily deceived and senseless— now calling to Egypt, now turning to Assyria" (Hosea 7:11).

The spirit of Ephraim is the spirit that finds fault with the LORD, it is a spirit that leads people to be disappointed with God because of the situation they find themselves in. It pushes people to look for help from the world, from the enemies of God. Many people are being deceived in the name of networking to form unholy alliances with the systems of this world. It is the spirit of an alternative. It seeks and employs alternatives to godly principles, and to God Himself. We will increasingly see even professing churches joining the woke culture which is the antichrist spirit disguised as social activism.

When you are in need do you wait for the salvation of the Lord or to you turn to Egypt and Assyria for help? The Lord spoke about those who readily seek for alternatives, in these words.

"Woe to the obstinate children," declares the Lord, "to those who carry out plans that are not mine, forming an alliance, but not by my Spirit, heaping sin upon sin; 2 who go down to Egypt without consulting me; who look for help to Pharaoh's protection, to Egypt's shade for refuge. 3 But Pharaoh's protection will be to your shame, Egypt's shade will bring you disgrace. 4 Though they have officials in Zoan and their envoys have arrived in Hanes, 5 everyone will be put to shame because of a people useless to them, who bring neither help nor advantage, but only shame and disgrace" (Isaiah 30:1-5).

The Lord frowns at His children when they form unholy alliances and look to the world for help. We are seeing these unholy alliances increasing all over, sometimes under the guise of unity.

How to defeat the tendency to look for alternatives
1. Understand alternatives are futile

Only that which is done by the Lord or with the Lord endures. The psalmist said, "Unless the Lord builds the house, the builders labor in vain. Unless the Lord watches over the city, the guards stand watch in vain. 2 In vain you rise early and stay up late, toiling for food to eat— for he grants sleep to those he loves" (Psalm 127:1-2). So, alternatives to God will only lead to vain labor.

2. Destroy the alternate bridges

Just like in the case of spiritual adultery, the secret here is to get rid of all alternatives. You will have to put all your eggs in the one basket of the Lord. Blow up all those alternate bridges

"As the eyes of slaves look to the hand of their master, as the eyes of a female slave look to the hand of her mistress, so our eyes look to the Lord our God, till he shows us his mercy" (Psalm 123:2).

Falsehood and deceit
"Whenever I would heal Israel, the sins of Ephraim are exposed and the crimes of Samaria revealed. They practice deceit, thieves break into houses, bandits rob in the streets; 2 but they do not realize that I remember all their evil deeds. Their sins engulf them; they are always before me" (Hosea 7:1-2).

"Ephraim has surrounded me with lies, Israel with deceit. And Judah is unruly against God, even against the faithful Holy One" (Hosea 11:12).

Integrity in speech and action is fast becoming a thing of the past. It is easy for people to mean one thing in their hearts and declare another with their mouths. A few of the ways in which people are increasingly embracing falsehood are:

- False titles
- False degrees
- False identities
- False documents
- False testimonies
- False marriages

We sing songs in "worship" that do not reflect our true commitment. We surround God with lies in high sounding but powerless prayers.

How to defeat the spirit of falsehood and deceit
One thing that causes people to resort to falsehood is the fear of suffering. This suffering might be a consequence of their actions or just a result of the circumstances of life. This takes us back to the issue of contentment. It also takes us to the issue of alternatives. When one stops trusting God for breakthrough, one resorts to underhanded means to attain it. To defeat this spirit of falsehood, one must grow in contentment and the ability to trust the Lord and wait for His timing.

Compromise and complacency

"Ephraim mixes with the nations; Ephraim is a flat loaf not turned over" (Hosea 7:8).

The curse of this end times is the tendency of wanting to be accepted by a renegade world system that vehemently opposes anything that truly has to do with Jesus Christ. This yearning for acceptance is pushing many on the bed of compromise with a corrupt world. Of course, when one lies on the bed of compromise with a wicked world, the result is complacency viz a viz the things of the Kingdom. Remember, the Lord Jesus Christ said, "from the days of John the Baptist until now the kingdom of heaven suffereth violence, and the violent take it by force" (Matthew 11:12, KJV).

The Kingdom advances through men and women who have learned the art of exerting spiritual violence. It is the spiritually violent who lay hold of the Kingdom and cause its advancement in this side of eternity. The Lord said of Moab,

> "Moab has been at rest from youth, like wine left on its dregs, not poured from one jar to another—she has not gone into exile. So she tastes as she did, and her aroma is unchanged. "[12] But days are coming," declares the Lord, "when I will send men who pour from pitchers, and they will pour her out; they will empty her pitchers and smash her jars" (Jerimiah 48:11-12).

How to defeat compromise and complacency
1. Be baptized with fire

Any living thing set on fire does not stay still. The heat of the fire keeps it moving. Position yourself for the baptism of fire and you will overcome the spirit of complacency. When you are baptized with fire, even if you want to compromise, things will refuse to stay close because of the heat of the fire you carry. That's why those baptized with fire find it difficult to compromise and be complacent.

2. Be consumed by zeal for His house

One natural effect of the baptism of fire is the zeal for the house of God. A heart aflame is a heart zealous for the things of the Kingdom of God. Paul exhorted us to, "Never be lacking in zeal, but keep your spiritual fervor, serving the Lord" (Romans 12:11). About the Messiah, it is written, "for zeal for your house consumes me" (Psalm 69:9). Let the zeal for His house consume you and you can't stay still.

3. Be poured out

To be poured out here means to move out of one's comfort and safety zone. When wine is in a bottle, it is locked up and safe. The danger of being spilled over comes in the process of being transferred from jar to jar. The transfer from jar to jar purifies the wine from the dregs and makes it fit for consumption. To be poured out is to become vulnerable but fit for consumption.

4. Be ready to stand alone if necessary

You must overcome the fear of standing alone if need be, if you must overcome compromise and complacency. There was a time when the Lord had to stand alone. There was a time when Paul stood alone. People of consequence often need to stand alone in order to avoid compromise and complacency.

Self-deception
"Foreigners sap his strength, but he does not realize it. His hair is sprinkled with gray, but he does not notice" (Hosea 7:9).

The danger of self-exaltation and being involved in everything is that the people around you are afraid to tell you the truth. When you always want to have the final word, people will let you have it in order to avoid trouble. So, even when you err no one dares tell you anything.

Sometimes there are changes in one's life that are obvious to others, but the individual concerned. These changes may involve one's looks, moral standards and other character issues. Everybody else sees what you are losing but because you are so self-deceived, blinded by your own greatness and importance, you are not able to take any notice. Ephraim was losing his strength to foreigners because of compromise without realizing it. There were physical changes in his life, unnoticed by him.

How to defeat self-deception

To defeat self-deception, one must embrace a meek and humble spirit, humility will make you open to the suggestions and opinions of others. It makes you treat everyone with respect. This makes the scale of blindness that leads to self-deception fall off one's eyes.

Hidden sins

"The iniquity of Ephraim is bound up; his sin is hid" (Hosea 13:12, KJV)

"Whenever I would heal Israel, the sins of Ephraim are exposed and the crimes of Samaria revealed. They practice deceit, thieves break into houses, bandits rob in the streets; 2 but they do not realize that I remember all their evil deeds. Their sins engulf them; they are always before me" (Hosea 7:1-2).

The spirit of Ephraim is a spirit that makes people cover and hide their sins instead of exposing and repenting from them. It makes people more concerned about their reputation and the opinion of people than about their salvation and freedom from bondage. In reality, it is the spirit of pride. Sins can be hidden for a time from fellow humans but never hidden from God. The question is what does God see concerning you? Does it agree with what humans see?

Defeating the tendency to hide one's own sins

To overcome this tendency to cover one's own sin, you must cease to depend on your self-righteousness and know that except on redemption ground, there is no righteousness or holiness in you. Understand that but for the redeeming grace of God, the heart of man is desperately corrupt and wicked, capable of anything. Rely on the holiness and righteousness of God, which Christ has become for you.

Chapter five

Deliverance from the spirit of Ephraim

In the first four chapters we looked at the different manifestations of the spirit of Ephraim and how we can defeat this spirit in our personal lives and help others to overcome it. In this chapter, we will look at how to receive total freedom from this spirit of Ephraim.

Because each of us has a blind spot in our lives where dangers lurk without our knowledge or ability to notice, it is essential to not make any assumptions and just pray against the different manifestations.

1. Plead the blood of Jesus on yourself spirit, soul, and body, family, property, job/ business/ ministry, finances etc.
2. Thank the Lord for His victory over the works of satan
3. Thank the Lord for His power available to set free captives
4. Ask the Lord to forgive you for any way you have allowed the spirit of Ephraim to operate in your life. It is advisable to pray through this list:

- The desire/passion to be involved in everything

- The incapacity to celebrate the success/victory of others in spite of you, even when it benefits you
- Deriving joy and satisfaction to have accomplished more than others
- Deriving satisfaction from being better than others
- The capacity to generate internal strife
- An attitude of entitlement
- Self-exaltation
- The inability to accept rejection without resorting to damage and destruction
- The inability to repent
- Envy
- Spiritual Adultery
- Looking to the world for remedy
- Falsehood and deceit
- Compromise and complacency
- Self-deception
- Hidden sins

5. Renounce these manifestations listed above and separate your heart from each.
6. Declare the victory of the cross over satan and his cohorts, and break every grip of the spirit of Ephraim over your life.
7. Now, by faith, bind and cast out the spirit of Ephraim from your life.

8. Proclaim your freedom from the spirit of Ephraim and thank the Lord for His victory in your life
9. Close every door in your life to this spirit and seal it with the blood of Jesus.

Part 2: The spirit of gehazi

Chapter six

Discerning and defeating the Spirit of Gehazi

The spirit of Gehazi is another subtle end-time spirit that masks itself in religious language, activism, and appearance. Gehazi, was serving a great Man of God, but he was of a different spirit from that of the man of God. He was always in the presence of this great man, but nothing of the prophet robbed over on Gehazi. In other words, he was always present but not connected.

Increasingly, we will see a great number of people in spiritual disconnect surround men and women of God. They will be physically present, outwardly committed, but truly disconnected in heart and soul. What are the manifestations of the spirit of Gehazi?

Judging by external appearances
It is a natural human tendency to judge by external appearances. Humanity focuses so much on what pleases the eye, the reason for all the charade we see everywhere. The Lord told the seasoned prophet Samuel, "Do not consider his appearance or his height, for I have rejected him. The Lord does not look at the things people look at. People look at the outward appearance, but the Lord looks at the heart" (1 Samuel 16:7).

The spirit of Gehazi takes this tendency to another dimension and even blinds its victims to that which does not meet the eyes.

This incapacity to see beyond the physical, makes people bypass their blessings and treat with disdain what they should be celebrating, while celebrating what should be on the dung heap. It makes people block access to what should be granted access and grants access to what shouldn't have access. This incapacity makes people embrace what they should run from and run from what they should be embracing.

If you look at 2 Kings 4:26-28, you see Gehazi being totally driven by external appearance in the way he handles this distressed lady. Although Gehazi was around the man of God, he was limited to the physical and external. He was willing to use brute force against this woman who was in great distress. Unlike the prophet who was able to sense in the spirit that this woman was in great distress, Gehazi was clueless. His actions were in response to physical manifestations.

Like Simon the leper who couldn't distinguish between an immoral touch and a touch of sincere worship when Mary knelt at the Master's feet, Gehazi took the woman's desperation for aggression.

Increasingly, we will see people who God has raised be surrounded by people who will prevent those in need from assessing the Man of God. In the name of bodyguards, these individuals will increasingly become gatekeepers who select who can reach the man of God and who cannot, based on who can afford a fee or what kind of car they drive or how well they are dressed up.

Nowadays, fraudsters with financial power have easier access to men of God than genuine believers who live in poverty. "Kingdom financiers" have more access to men of God than church workers. This is the influence of the spirit of Gehazi. God really needs to help us! It was easier to access the Lord Jesus and the prophets in the Bible than it is to do so the men of God of our time, especially when you are not economically privileged. Because of this increased focus on the external, people will become more vulnerable to the wiles of satan and his cohorts.

How to overcome this tendency to focus on the external
1. Be spiritually minded

When you are spiritually minded you act based on the fact that there is more to life than what meets the eyes. You tend to look at even trivial things from the perspective of the spirit. It makes you look with the eyes of the heart and hear with the ears of the heart than you do with the physical senses.

2. Make no judgment of things or people than what the spirit of God says

Of the Lord Jesus Christ, it is said that "He will not judge by what he sees with his eyes, or decide by what he hears with his ears" (Isaiah 11:3b). During His earthly ministry, He told the Jews to "Stop judging by mere appearances, but instead judge correctly" (John 7:24). When you limit your judgements to external appearances or words, you are making wrong judgement calls. Why? Because appearances can be very deceptive, and the devil is master at mimicking appearances.

Spiritual disconnect

When misfortune struck this lady through the sudden death of her miracle boy, the prophet Elisha commissioned Gehazi with his staff to go and raise the boy. 2 Kings 4:29-31 lets us know that Gehazi went but could not produce the results. He couldn't raise the boy even though he had the staff of the prophet with him. This shows that although Gehazi was always with Elisha, he never laid hold of the spirit of Elisha.

It is a spiritual principle that the anointing robs over when one is connected to an anointed person. Physical contact is not a guarantee of connectedness. Gehazi was always in contact with the anointed but was bereft of the anointing. Connection is something of the heart and spirit. That is why even people who are connected from a distance can tap into the graces of the man of God while those physically present, but disconnected, do not lay hold of it.

He had the staff of the prophet, was commissioned by him, but he could not fulfill the commission because of spiritual disconnect. There are several ways this spiritual disconnect will manifest these last days. Increasingly, we will see individuals who "have lost connection with the head, from whom the whole body, supported and held together by its ligaments and sinews" (Colossians 2:19) do the following:

Institutionalize religious festivities

"Therefore do not let anyone judge you by what you eat or drink, or with regard to a religious festival, a New Moon celebration or a Sabbath day" (Colossians 2:16).

The spirit of Gehazi is going to cause people to chase shadows and abandon the substance. We will increasingly see men of God, controlled by the spirit of Gehazi lead their followers into institutionalized religious festivities, and people will be forced to partake or be written off.

Worship spiritual experiences

> "Do not let anyone who delights in false humility and the worship of angels disqualify you. Such a person also goes into great detail about what they have seen; they are puffed up with idle notions by their unspiritual mind" (Colossians 2:18).

Take a look at the church landscape today and you immediately notice that fewer churches that emphasize the teaching of scripture and spiritual knowledge attract as many believers compared to those that parade "signs and wonders". I am not saying there should be a divide between solid teaching of scriptures and the performance of signs and wonders. However, where there are counterfeit manifestations of signs and wonders, there is usually an absence of the sound teaching of the unadulterated word of God.

People rather flock to where they hear made up stories, or where people go into great details to describe their spiritual experiences rather than teaching sound doctrine. This, too, is a sign of spiritual disconnect.

Substitute the leadership of the Spirit with rules and regulations

"[20] Since you died with Christ to the elemental spiritual forces of this world, why, as though you still belonged to the world, do you submit to its rules: [21] "Do not handle! Do not taste! Do not touch!"? [22] These rules, which have to do with things that are all destined to perish with use, are based on merely human commands and teachings. [23] Such regulations indeed have an appearance of wisdom, with their self-imposed worship, their false humility and their harsh treatment of the body, but they lack any value in restraining sensual indulgence" (Colossians 2:20-23).

Rather than teach and equip people on how to live by the Spirit, the spirit of Gehazi tries to get people abide by external rules whether written or implied. People will no longer be thought to develop the spiritual senses and live by their convictions. The spirit of Gehazi will encourage people to seek the 'prophets' for their decision making.

How to overcome spiritual disconnect
1. Be filled with the Holy Spirit

When you are filled with the Holy Spirit and get refilled, you stay connected to the head who is Christ Jesus.

2. Be sincere in your associations

There is no need to be physically present when your heart is not connected to the one who matters. Probably Gehazi was in for what he could get by being around the man of God not because his destiny had to do with the man of God. Avoid anything that will make you be halfhearted in your dealing with people.

Chapter Seven

Discerning and defeating the spirit of Gehazi – 2

In this chapter, like the previous one, we will continue our study of the manifestations of the spirit of Gehazi and how we can defeat it in our lives.

Covetousness

"One day Elisha went to Shunem. And a well-to-do woman was there, who urged him to stay for a meal. So whenever he came by, he stopped there to eat. [9] She said to her husband, "I know that this man who often comes our way is a holy man of God. [10] Let's make a small room on the roof and put in it a bed and a table, a chair and a lamp for him. Then he can stay there whenever he comes to us" (2Kings 4:8-11).

I want you to note that Elisha did not ask the woman for anything, she constraint him to stay for a meal. It was the woman's initiative to be a blessing to the man of God. We have Gehazis going around and asking people for handsome seeds in exchange for miracles. Beware of prophets who ask for monetary or material values in exchange for miracles. Such are motivated by the spirit of covetousness. Usually, they cite the example of Elijah and the widow to justify their covetousness.

We know for sure that God expressly asked Elijah to go to the widow and be fed. My question to such people is, "did the word of the Lord come to you asking you to go ask for the seed you are requesting?"

Another thing to note from the passage is that the woman perceived that Elisha was a holy man of God, and served him in line with her perception. What I mean is that what you are in the heart will be communicated to your environment. If you are a covetous man of God, people will offer you money or material things. If you are immoral man of God, people will offer you sex. Whatever you are made of in the inside will be communicated to the outside.

People tend to offer you what they think will promote who you are, as perceived by them. This holy man of God was offered a place to meet God. He was offered a retreat apartment so to speak. The contents of the room tell us we do not need sophistication for divine encounters. There are servants of God who demand to be hosted in five-star hotels before they can accept to minister. A quiet room in someone's home was enough for Elisha.

Gehazi did not learn from his master's simplicity. The passage in 2Kings 5:21-27 shows us how far people influenced by this spirit are willing to go, to satisfy their lust for material things.

> "So Gehazi hurried after Naaman. When Naaman saw him running toward him, he got down from the chariot to meet him. "Is everything all right?" he asked. 22 "Everything is all right,"

Gehazi answered. "My master sent me to say, 'Two young men from the company of the prophets have just come to me from the hill country of Ephraim. Please give them a talent of silver and two sets of clothing.'"

23 "By all means, take two talents," said Naaman. He urged Gehazi to accept them, and then tied up the two talents of silver in two bags, with two sets of clothing. He gave them to two of his servants, and they carried them ahead of Gehazi. 24 When Gehazi came to the hill, he took the things from the servants and put them away in the house. He sent the men away and they left. 25 When he went in and stood before his master, Elisha asked him, "Where have you been, Gehazi?" "Your servant didn't go anywhere," Gehazi answered. 26 But Elisha said to him, "Was not my spirit with you when the man got down from his chariot to meet you? Is this the time to take money or to accept clothes—or olive groves and vineyards, or flocks and herds, or male and female slaves? 27 Naaman's leprosy will cling to you and to your descendants forever." Then Gehazi went from Elisha's presence and his skin was leprous—it had become as white as snow" (2Kings 5:21-27).

From the above passage we can bring out the following characteristics or the manifestation of covetousness:

Manifestations of covetousness
Willingness to tell lies for material gain

Gehazi ran after Naaman and told a lie that he had been sent by Elisha. Covetousness will push a lot of people to become false to themselves and to others for the sake of material gain.

Fabrication of stories and testimonies for the sake material gain

Ghazi did not only tell a lie, he fabricated a testimony for the sake of material gain. He was willing to use the work of God to indulge his lust. He said "two young men from the company of prophets…please give them". In a similar way, people possessed by the spirit of Gehazi will make request for donations on behalf of the people of God and the work of God and use it for their personal interests. The work of God or the workers in the vineyard are just vehicles for them to use to amass personal fortunes. If you think you have seen anything, watch and see as this becomes more blatant.

Duplicity

Gehazi came back from his mission of covetousness and stood before Elisha as though nothing had happened. He even lied again, to the man of God, that he had not been anywhere. Covetousness makes you act one way before one set of people to gain their favor and act another way before another set of people to gain their favor. To them the end justifies the means. People controlled by the spirit of Gehazi cannot differentiate running after the world for favors and gain, and standing before God. To them it is the same; serving the god of marmon and serving the Omnipotent God.

Merchandizing the power of God

While this wasn't directly done by Gehazi, it is an extension of his spirit. In the midst of a revival in Samaria, accompanied by a demonstration of the power of God, a young convert offered the apostles money in exchange for importation. However, Peter would have none of that:

"When Simon saw that the Spirit was given at the laying on of the apostles' hands, he offered them money [19] and said, "Give me also this ability so that everyone on whom I lay my hands may receive the Holy Spirit" (Acts 8:18-19).

Today, servants of God are accepting, and even demanding, offers from the likes of Simons, and imparting them with the gifts and power of God. This is done under the guise of partnership and special circles. Is it any doubt that sorcerers have taken over the pulpit? May the Lord help his servants, like Peter, to see beyond the charade:

[20] "Peter answered: "May your money perish with you, because you thought you could buy the gift of God with money! [21] You have no part or share in this ministry, because your heart is not right before God" (Acts 8:20-21).

Think of it, what would have happened had Peter not discern the spirit behind Simon's request? He would have imparted a man "full of bitterness and captive to sin" (v 23). Today Simons are multiplying on the pulpit and demonstrating the power of God, yet they are full of bitterness and captive to the sin of covetousness, because there are people God anointed with power who are now serving the God of marmon, and ordaining their likes.

How to defeat covetousness
1. Set your heart on things above

"Since, then, you have been raised with Christ, set your hearts on things above, where Christ is, seated at the right hand of God" (Colossians 3:1).

The easiest way to set your heart on the things above is to invest your treasures in the things above. The Lord Jesus said,

> "Do not store up for yourselves treasures on earth, where moths and vermin destroy, and where thieves break in and steal. [20] But store up for yourselves treasures in heaven, where moths and vermin do not destroy, and where thieves do not break in and steal. [21] For where your treasure is, there your heart will be also" (Matthew 19-21).

When you amass treasures on earth, the tendency is to want to see the treasures increase. The more you keep the more you want. The more you transfer to the other side of eternity the less you want for yourself.

2. Set your mind on things above

"Set your minds on things above, not on earthly things" (Colossians 3:2).

When the mind is set on earthly things, it devises earthly means to acquire more earthly things. When the mind is set on things above, it receives inspiration for heavenly pursuits.

3. Let Christ Jesus be enough for you

When the rich young ruler came to Jesus. The Lord asked him to go sell all he has and come follow Him. Jesus is enough for those who truly follow Him. Not Jesus plus fame or riches or power or material possessions. To heal your heart from covetousness, you may need to "sell all you have" so you can truly follow Jesus and Him alone.

Spiritual "parasiting"

A spiritual parasite is someone who attaches himself/herself to a spiritual person/environment for material gain. Such an individual may act spiritual, speak spiritual, look spiritual but his/her heart and eyes are set only on the material and earthly benefits such association brings. This is another manifestation of the spirit of Gehazi.

When the man of God Elisha went to glory, one would have thought Gehazi would continue the ministry of his master like Elisha did that of Elijah. However, this was not the case. Because of the spiritual disconnect and covetousness, Gehazi could not continue with the ministry. He was a spiritual parasite. He was using his association with the prophet to gain access to high places. We saw how he used his association with the prophet to extort Naaman after he was healed of his leprosy.

The next time we hear of Gehazi, it is when he was in the courts of the king and narrating to him some of the exploits of Elisha. Even after the death of the man of God, Gehazi was still using his name to gain access to high places.

> "The king was talking to Gehazi, the servant of the man of God, and had said, "Tell me about all the great things Elisha has done." 5 Just as Gehazi was telling the king how Elisha had restored the dead to life, the woman whose son Elisha had brought back to life came to appeal to the king for her house and land" (2 Kings 8:4-6).

What was Gehazi doing in the king's court? Why isn't there anything with respect to the ministry of Elisha written about Gehazi considering the fact that he was the personal assistant to the anointed man of God? The only thing he continued was to have access to high places by association with the anointed, not for spiritual reasons but for material benefit. Gehazi did not continue the ministry of Elisha, but continued exploiting the connections he had established by serving the prophet. He was using his knowledge of the exploits of the Man of God for personal material benefit.

Permit ask you some questions: Why are you around that man or woman of God? Why are you serving him or her? Is there s spiritual bonding between you and him/her?

Someone might say because Elisha cursed Gehazi with leprosy he could not have continued the ministry. I want to disagree! Gehazi could not have been in the palace of the king, let alone talking face to face with him, if he still had leprosy. I strongly believe, although not recorded, that Elisha had compassion on Gehazi and healed him of his leprosy

The remedies that we have applied to the other manifestations of the spirit of Gehazi will apply also to spiritual "parasiting".

Chapter Eight

Deliverance from the spirit of Gehazi

1. Plead the blood of Jesus on yourself spirit, soul, and body, family, property, job/ business/ ministry, finances etc.
2. Thank the Lord for His victory over the works of satan
3. Thank the Lord for His power available to set free captives
4. Ask the Lord to forgive you for anyway you have allowed the spirit of gehazi to operate in your life. It is advisable to pray through this list:
   - Judging by external appearances
   - Walking in the flesh
   - Spiritual disconnect
   - Covetousness
   - Spiritual "parasiting"
5. Renounce these manifestations listed above and separate your heart from each.
6. Declare the victory of the cross over satan and his cohorts, and break every grip of the spirit of gehazi over your life.
7. Now, by faith, bind and cast out the spirit of gehazi from your life.
8. Proclaim your freedom from the spirit of gehazi and thank the Lord for His victory in your life

9. Close every door in your life to this spirit and seal it with the blood of Jesus.

Part 3: The spirit of Jezebel

Chapter Nine

Discerning and defeating the spirit of Jezebel

The first mention of Jezebel in the Bible occurs in 1 Kings 16:31, where she is mentioned as the wife of Ahab. "He not only considered it trivial to commit the sins of Jeroboam son of Nebat, but he also married Jezebel daughter of Ethbaal king of the Sidonians, and began to serve Baal and worship him" (1 Kings 16:31).

The name Jezebel means "Baal exalts" or "Baal is husband to" or "unchaste". The spirit of Jezebel is the spirit that seeks to make people depend on the demon god called baal. This spirit brings people into spiritual union with baal, and promotes unchastity both among the single or married. In other words, it is the spirit of sexual promiscuity and vanity.

Jezebel was daughter of Ethbaal which means "with Baal", "living with Baal", or "enjoying the favor and help of Baal". Her father was the priest of baal who lived with baal and enjoyed the favor of baal. We can see here that the spirit of jezebel is the spirit of baal in female form. She is raised by baal, married to baal, enjoys the favor of baal, and is with baal. Her origins, her being, and her future are all in baal.

Just like the original Jezebel, there are many young women moving about in human flesh but who's origins are in baal. That is, they have been raised by baal, equipped, and send into the world to destroy destinies. Because they are married to baal, they are portals through which his spirit comes among humans in order to take them captive and make them serve baal. In these last days we will see a multiplication of the activities of the spirit of jezebel and the spirit of baal. They often go together. Let us examine the manifestations of this spirit and see how we can defeat it in our lives and environment.

How the spirit manifests
It kills the genuine prophetic

"Haven't you heard, my lord, what I did while Jezebel was killing the prophets of the Lord? I hid a hundred of the Lord's prophets in two caves, fifty in each, and supplied them with food and water" (1Kings 18:13).

The spirit of jezebel is a spirit that kills the prophets of God both physically and spiritually. It hates the prophetic because the genuine prophetic exposes her activities and is the only force able to counter her moves. Just like she did in the days she physically walked this earth, the spirit of jezebel is still killing prophets.

I don't know how and why she succeeds in killing the prophets, but the Lord lets it happen. That is why we read about mystery Babylon,

"In her was found the blood of prophets and of God's holy people, of all who have been slaughtered on the earth" (Revelations 18:24). It is through the activities of the spirit of Jezebel that the blood of prophets is shed. Like I said earlier, this killing might be spiritual also. In other words, she kills the gift instead of the individual. How does she kill the gift?

The spirit of jezebel kills the prophetic gift by stealing it from those ordained by God as prophets and transferring it to those she has ordained as her own prophets. It also kills by contaminating the gift beyond recovery such that it can only serve the purposes of baal. This leads us to the next characteristic.

It is the matron spirit of false prophets

The spirit of Jezebel is the matron spirit of the false prophets. While it seeks to destroy genuine prophets, it also works to raise a plethora of false prophets who do her bidding. As we see the activities of the jezebel spirit multiplying in these last days, so shall we see the activities of the counterfeit prophetic increasing exponentially.

False prophets are not necessarily those who make prophesies that do not come to fulfilment, but they are people who prophesy by the spirit of baal. Sometimes their prophecies may come to fulfilment, but the spirit behind such prophecies is not the Spirit of Jesus Christ. Usually, the aim of such prophecies is to lead the people of God away from trusting in the Lord only to trusting in human beings and the objects they promote. Simply put, the spirit of jezebel is there to promote idolatry (see 1 Kings 18:18, 1 Kings 19).

It is a spirit of fear and intimidation

> "Now Ahab told Jezebel everything Elijah had done and how he had killed all the prophets with the sword. ² So Jezebel sent a messenger to Elijah to say, 'May the gods deal with me, be it ever so severely, if by this time tomorrow I do not make your life like that of one of them.'³ Elijah was afraid[a] and ran for his life. When he came to Beersheba in Judah, he left his servant there, ⁴ while he himself went a day's journey into the wilderness. He came to a broom bush, sat down under it and prayed that he might die. "I have had enough, Lord," he said. "Take my life; I am no better than my ancestors." ⁵ Then he lay down under the bush and fell asleep" (1 Kings 19:1-3).

The spirit of Jezebel is also the spirit of fear and intimidation. When someone with the spirit of Jezebel speaks, they have an unusual capacity to release the spirit of fear into their hearers. It doesn't matter whether they hear it directly or indirectly. Jezebel only sent a message to the great prophet, it was a relayed message, yet it still instilled fear and panic in the prophet.

People operating with the sprit of Jezebel have the tendency to bring unholy fear in others. They speak to intimidate. Even their well-intended actions and words have the capacity to instill fear. When they try to motivate, they do so by instilling fear. This spirit will increasingly be employed by leaders, and governments as we enter the final stages of the end-times. The goal of the weapon of fear is to manipulate and control others. This leads us to our next characteristic of the spirit of Jezebel.

It is the spirit of manipulation and control

(see 1 Kings 21)

The spirit of Jezebel uses fear to manipulate and control people. As narrated in the passage in 1 Kings 21, we see how Jezebel manipulated and controlled her husband Ahab to perform her evil schemes. Not only did she manipulate her husband, but she did the entire leadership of a whole city to murder an innocent man. We will see the spirit increasingly manipulate leadership of churches, cities, and even nations to do the bidding of baal.

This spirit uses every method to gain what it wants irrespective of the damage caused to people or property. It will even use biblical principles in a manipulative way. We will see it take over pulpits and ministries to manipulate the people of God. People who love the Lord and obey His Word will be primary targets. The spirit of Jezebel will manipulate scriptures to manipulate those who are not watchful and lack divine wisdom.

See how many people give because of manipulation by some masters of psychological mind games, and then turn and discredit the gospel of Christ. If they gave out of conviction by the Holy Spirit, there would be no regrets, but the joy of giving that lasts for eternity will fill their hearts.

How to defeat the afore listed manifestation of the spirit of jezebel

How do you overcome this spirit of fear, manipulation, control and false prophets?

1. Develop a sound knowledge of scripture

False prophets prey on people based on their ignorance of the Holy Scriptures. When they notice that you lack adequate knowledge of what the word of God says, they immediately resort to twist the scriptures. Remember how satan tried to twist the scriptures when he tempted our Lord? in the same way false prophets make scriptures say or imply what it doesn't say or imply.

2. Sharpen your spiritual senses

When your spiritual senses are up and running, especially the senses of sight, sound, and smell, you can easily see, hear, or smell manipulative tendencies and guard against them.

3. Be conscious of the Lord your shield and refuge

"The Lord is my light and my salvation— whom shall I fear?
The Lord is the stronghold of my life— of whom shall I be afraid?
² When the wicked advance against me to devour me, it is my enemies and my foes who will stumble and fall. ³ Though an army besiege me, my heart will not fear; though war break out against me, even then I will be confident" (Psalm 27:1-3).

David's consciousness of the Lord as his protector made him fearless and unafraid of anything- he was so sure of his divine refuge and shield that he found no reason to fear or be afraid. You need to resolve in your heart to not fear anything or anyone but God.

Chapter Ten

Discerning and defeating the spirit of Jezebel - 2

In this chapter, we continue to examine the spirit of Jezebel.

Further manifestations of the spirit of jezebel
It sends the genuine prophets into hiding

The spirit of Jezebel is a spirit that sends genuine prophets of God into hiding. When it cannot kill the prophets, it makes them go into hiding. This hiding can be both spiritual and physical. This is achieved by covering the star of the prophet and causing them to not discover who they are or through fear, intimidation, manipulation and control. Jezebel made the great prophet Elijah went to hide in a cave. She also forced 100 prophets to hide in a cave in fear for their lives.

When one lives in a cave long enough, he or she tends to develop a cave mentality. When you are in a cave your vision is narrow and blurred. You tend to see only the things that are around you, that is, your visibility range is severely limited. It is the spirit of Jezebel that makes these prophets to be concerned only about the things very close to them and the things which bring only temporary rewards. They have lost the light of eternity and the rewards it holds. They seem to live for now and want their best life now. That's how powerful the spirit of Jezebel can be if you let it. Because it is the spirit that drives genuine prophets into hiding in caves, it is the spirit of frustration, depression, and resignation.

It is the spirit of frustration depression, and resignation

We will increasingly see ministers of the gospel resigning from pursuing the higher calling out of frustration and depression. We will also see ordinary Christians giving up on their faith out of frustration and depression because of the difficulty they are encountering. All this will be due to the increase in activity of the spirit of Jezebel.

Remember when the great prophet Elijah decided that he had had enough and wanted to die? That was the spirit of suicide arising out of depression, frustration, and a sense of resignation. We will see even young people who have opened themselves to this spirit decide to end their own lives because of the hopelessness the spirit of jezebel is instilling in them.

Think of how the minds of young people are constantly bombarded with computer generated shapes and figures. See how they are being encouraged to pursue ideals they will never attain. See how society is shaping them to believe that their lives are only worth the flashy things they can possess. See how they are being encouraged to hate who God made them to be and transition to something else they will never become.

The pursuit of such illusions is encouraged by this spirit of fear, intimidation, control and manipulation, and the end result is suicide.

It is the spirit of vanity, immorality, and seduction

"Then Jehu went to Jezreel. When Jezebel heard about it, she put on eye makeup, arranged her hair and looked out of a window" (2 Kings 9:30).

Vanity in looks and appearances is the handiwork of the spirit of Jezebel. So many people are being initiated into baal worship because of vanity products they purchased from agents of Jezebel and use on themselves without praying over them. Many of the makeup products you see in the marketplace have their origins from the underworld where jezebel is queen.

Just by using such products individuals open themselves up to spirits of sexual immorality and perversion and hence become agents of seduction. Haven't you heard people complaining that immoral individuals are trying to connect with them. Many times they are not aware that the vanity facial, hair, and other cosmetic products they purchase carried spirits of seduction.

There is a makeup a woman wears which makes her seductive. There are hairdos made to arouse sexual desire. There are perfumes worn that makes the members of the opposite sex feel aroused when they smell it. The actions of Jezebel cited above were intended to seduce Jehu, but thank God he was a man of singular focus.

It is the spirit that causes doctrinal error

"Nevertheless, I have this against you: You tolerate that woman Jezebel, who calls herself a prophet. By her teaching she misleads my servants into sexual immorality and the eating of food sacrificed to idols" (Revelations 2:20).

One of the characteristics of false prophets is their ability to introduce false and misleading teachings. Jezebel here called herself a prophet. As a result of her teachings genuine servants of Christ Jesus were led into sexual immorality and the worship of idols. Take a look at the church landscape today and you notice a lot of false doctrines that seem to promote sin and sinful compromise. The spirit of Jezebel is the spirit of heresy.

Some propagate this heretical teachings out of ignorance and deception, others out of design to lead as many people astray as possible. Remember we said earlier that the spirit of jezebel seeks to get people to serve baal. Jezebel is baal's evangelist and prophet.

How to overcome the spirit of jezebel
1. Live in healthy connection with likeminded others

One of the reasons Elijah resigned because of threats from jezebel is because he thought, he was the only one serving the Lord who remained in all Israel. In his mind, if jezebel had succeeded to eliminate everyone else, then she would succeed to eliminate him. When you think you are standing alone, you are less likely to resist the enemy onslaught. It is very likely that Elijah, lived in some form of isolation and unhealthy disconnect. God had to remind him that there were seven thousand who like him had not bowed the knee to baal.

2. Put your hope in God only

The Bible says, "Hope deferred makes the heart sick, but a longing fulfilled is a tree of life" (Proverbs 13:12). Be satisfied with Christ Jesus. Put all your hope in Him so that you do not become frustrated, disappointed, and depressed. For "no one who hopes in you will ever be put to shame" (Psalm 25:3).

3. Pray over everything you get from the marketplace

We said the markets are flooded with articles from the underworld ruled by the spirit of jezebel. Anyone who buys and uses such articles become a victim of that spirit. However, since you cannot manufacture everything you genuinely need, make sure to pray for everything before and after purchase. This will shield you from opening any door into your life to the Jezebel spirit.

Chapter eleven

Deliverance from the spirit of Jezebel

Like every other demonic spirit, the spirit of Jezebel has several portals through which it can take control of an individual. One of these portals is the ancestral portal. If any of your ancestors was raised by, worshipped, or enjoyed the favor of baal, your life is an easy access to the spirit of jezebel. Another portal is your own actions.

It could be something you purchased and used which was from the underworld ruled by the jezebel spirit. Or you may have developed a tendency to manipulate or control others. This has likely opened your life to the spirit of jezebel which is a spirit of witchcraft.

Very close associations with those inhabited by the spirit of jezebel can also open you up to that spirit. If you have ever consulted a false prophet or stayed under his/her teaching, or used any material from such an individual, you have likely opened your life to this demonic spirit. Whatever portal the spirit used to enter you, it can be cast out in the Name and power of Jesus Christ.

1. Pray and cover yourself, family, property, business etc. an everything that concerns or is related to you with the blood of Jesus.
2. Thank the Lord for His power and victory over the devil and his collaborators
3. Repent for any of the manifestations or characteristics of this spirit that you see in your life. again, because most people do not really know themselves, it is advisable to pray through the list:
   - frustration
   - depression,
   - resignation
   - vanity,
   - immorality,
   - seduction
   - manipulation
   - control
   - doctrinal error
   - patronizing false prophets
   - receiving ministry from false prophets
   - fear
   - intimidation
4. Renounce all of the manifestations and separate yourself spirit, soul and body from them.

5. Command, in the Name of Jesus, the spirit of jezebel to come of your life and never to return
6. Declare your freedom from the spirit of jezebel.
7. Close the doors to that spirit and seal it with the blood of Jesus
8. Thank the Lord for your deliverance

Part 4: The spirit of Judas Iscariot

Chapter Twelve

Discerning and defeating the spirit of Judas Iscariot – 1

The spirit of Judas Iscariot is primarily the spirit of disloyalty and betrayal. Scripture in general, and the Lord Jesus in particular, had much to say about this spirit as an end time spirit.

> "Therefore in the east give glory to the Lord; exalt the name of the Lord, the God of Israel, in the islands of the sea. [16] From the ends of the earth we hear singing: "Glory to the Righteous One." But I said, "I waste away, I waste away! Woe to me! The treacherous betray! With treachery the treacherous betray!" [17] Terror and pit and snare await you, people of the earth" (Isaiah 24:15-17).

One of the marks of the end times is that the Gospel will spread and be proclaimed across the globe, from the east to the west, north to south, people will increasingly praise and worship the God if Israel. There will be mighty sounds of genuine praise and worship to the God who created the heavens and the earth. Even as the sound of worship rises to the throne and the Gospel of Christ Jesus is proclaimed, there will be increase in betrayal. The treacherous will increasingly become more brazen in their attempts to betray their own in all spheres of society. The prophet prophesied terror and pit and snare to the people of the earth. Let us look at some areas in which this will be very common.

Where it will manifest
Within families

"Brother will betray brother to death, and a father his child; children will rebel against their parents and have them put to death" (Matthew 10:21).

The spirit of Judas Iscariot will increasingly take its grip within families. We are going to see an increase in the level with which family members will resort to betraying one another, if people do not consciously guard against this end time spirits. As society undermines family values and produces a generation of young men and women who subscribe more to certain ideologies than they do to their families, family relationships will become increasingly worthless. The loyalty and dedication that should be ascribed to one's relatives will be transferred to organizations and systems that promote certain ideologies.

We are already seeing this manifesting. Parents are murdering their own offspring for the pleasure of it because they subscribe to the ideology of choice. Children are rising up against their parents and putting them to death. Siblings are turning against one another for different reasons.

Within congregations

"At that time many will turn away from the faith and will betray and hate each other, [11] and many false prophets will appear and deceive many people" (Matthew 24:10).

"You will be betrayed even by parents, brothers and sisters, relatives and friends, and they will put some of you to death" (Luke 21:16).

Even as there will be a great falling away from the faith as people abandon the way of the cross and embrace apparently sophisticated philosophies, they will become bitter and angry at those who still uphold the values of the cross of Christ. This anger and bitterness will turn to hatred because they will embrace the lie that true believers are the obstacle to tolerance and equity. In these days of the great deception, only those who hold tight to the cross of Christ and the word of God will be able to see through the duplicity and sound the alarm bells. In doing so they are drawing the indignation of those who take the bait, line and sinker.

Between friends

"Beware of your friends; do not trust anyone in your clan. For every one of them is a deceiver, and every friend a slanderer. [5] Friend deceives friend, and no one speaks the truth. They have taught their tongues to lie; they weary themselves with sinning" (Jerimiah 9:4-5).

The spirit of Judas Iscariot will not only invade families, and congregations, but will also invade social relationships like friendships.

People will become untrue to their friends, and because of selfish ambition will resort to falsehood and deception. They will flatter each other while at the same time they slander the ones they flatter.

Look at what the Psalmist said about this, in his case it was someone who was both a friend and a brother in the faith. We can say it was one with whom he had a covenant friendship.

> "If an enemy were insulting me, I could endure it; if a foe were rising against me, I could hide. [13] But it is you, a man like myself, my companion, my close friend, [14] with whom I once enjoyed sweet fellowship at the house of God, as we walked about among the worshipers... My companion attacks his friends; he violates his covenant. [21] His talk is smooth as butter, yet war is in his heart; his words are more soothing than oil, yet they are drawn swords" (Psalm 55:12-13, 20-21).

Those who will rise against you in these last days are not those you have perceived as enemies. It will be those you have considered close friends and companions. The very ones with whom you have had close fellowship in the house of God. It will be those you think you are in a covenant relationship with. People will increasingly disregard agreements and violate covenants they have established.

Between marriage partners

One relationship which is entirely based on a covenant before God is the relationship of matrimony. Even here the level of betrayal will increase. We have seen people resorting to breaking the marriage covenant for very silly reasons. In fact, society seems to applaud those who take steps to ditch their spouses for any and every reason. Living conditions and people's mindsets are being programmed to make it easier for spouses to betray one another's trust and their marriage vows.

Chapter Thirteen

Reasons why people will betray each other

In the last chapter we looked at areas in which this spirit of betrayal is going to be at work. We saw that, it will take roots in homes, in the church, and in social relationships. The reasons for this increase in betrayal are very diverse. In this chapter we look at some of the reasons people are increasingly going to resort to betraying one another.

For financial and material gain

"What are you willing to give me if I deliver him over to you?" So they counted out for him thirty pieces of silver" (Matthew 26:15).

Financial and material gain will be the paramount reason for the increased betrayal we will see in these last days. As people are increasingly programmed to worship the god of marmom, they will be ready to do anything to obtain more of it. Judas was willing to sell his maters for money. Delilah betrayed her lover Samson for silver. Children will betray their parents to receive quick inheritances. Spouses will divorce each other for the sake of alimony and other financial and material benefits.

Look at the landscape of society today, it is very likely that you know someone who has mysteriously lost a loved one and suddenly became rich. Many young people are into occultic societies and white lodges which lavish them with wealth and material things at the price of the life of a loved one. What a betrayal of the bond of kinhood. In Africa they call them ritualists. People who are ready to sacrifice family members or friends for the purpose of getting rich fast.

Here in the Western societies, it is much more subtle. People join these secret societies and white lodges to obtain wealth in exchange of their own destinies or the destinies and lives of loved ones. Because the population is rather ignorant of, and insensitive to, the spiritual things taking place in their environment, they are largely unaware of what is happening. There are things a man who is spiritual alive will see and immediately know what is in play here which others will never know. Believe me, these ritual killings do take place here too.

For promotion, position, and power

For power and position that they would otherwise not attain, people will increasingly betray others who have trusted them. There are organizations, and even governments where betrayal is the currency to rise to positions of power and influence. People of integrity and impeccable loyalty just cannot function or amount to anything within such organizations or governments. There was such a man in the Bible called Doeg, an official of Saul. From a simple shepherd he rose through the ranks using the currency of betrayal. Of him the psalmist said, "Here now is the man who did not make God his stronghold but trusted in his great wealth and grew strong by destroying others!" (Psalm 52:7).

For provision/survival

There is a conscious design to make life barely affordable for the greater part of the human population. The middle class is systematically being destroyed and there are multitudes who can't even meet their most basic needs. Some who used to live comfortably are now in a position where they can do anything to survive or return to their former status. Because of this, many people will be very open to be agents through which the enemy will destroy many with the weapon of betrayal. They will be forced to do it in order to survive. Intimate information about people will be sold to those profiteering from the gossip industry.

We see a case of betrayal for survival in the story of an Egyptian servant of Amalekite military officer. When David was going to fight alongside the Philistines against Israel, he was asked to return home by the philistine leadership. By the time he and his men got to their village, it had been raided and burnt to the ground by a raiding band. David inquired of God if he should pursue the enemy and the Lord said he should. Here is part of the story as they embarked on the pursuit:

> "They found an Egyptian in a field and brought him to David. They gave him water to drink and food to eat— [12] part of a cake of pressed figs and two cakes of raisins. He ate and was revived,

for he had not eaten any food or drunk any water for three days and three nights. ¹³ David asked him, "Who do you belong to? Where do you come from?" He said, "I am an Egyptian, the slave of an Amalekite. My master abandoned me when I became ill three days ago. ¹⁴ We raided the Negev of the Kerethites, some territory belonging to Judah and the Negev of Caleb. And we burned Ziklag."¹⁵ David asked him, "Can you lead me down to this raiding party?" He answered, "Swear to me before God that you will not kill me or hand me over to my master, and I will take you down to them." ¹⁶ He led David down, and there they were, scattered over the countryside, eating, drinking and reveling because of the great amount of plunder they had taken from the land of the Philistines and from Judah (1 Samuel 30:11-16).

Here is a typical scenario of betrayal and counter betrayal. The first betrayal came from the master of the servant. Because he did not want to give up some of the plunder he had taken, he considered his sick servant a burden and a risk, and abandoned him in the fields to die. For his personal survival he left behind a fellow soldier. I am sure as the young man lay there, abandoned to die, he felt disappointed and betrayed by his very own. He was in a dire situation and felt that he owed his life to this man who had attended to him. He then divulged classified information to David and his men. He knew the ins and out of his fellow soldiers who had betrayed him.

In exchange for his survival, he gave David the information he needed. He did not only give David information, but personally led the way to his master and his men, with guarantee that David wouldn't hand him over. His was a need for double survival; from the dire situation he was in at the time, and from slavery to his master.

Just out of hatred and jealousy

The story of Joseph and his brothers is one familiar to most of us. He was betrayed and sold into Egypt by his own brothers just out of jealousy. His dreams and special treatment he received from his father made the others become jealous to the point where they wanted him dead. While he came to them to seek their welfare, they bound him and dumped him into a pit to die. Selling him was just an opportunity they used to avoid the guilt of shedding his blood. Similarly in these last days we will see an increase in betrayal out of hatred and jealousy.

We see this also in the relationship between Jacob and his brother Esau. Because of longstanding anger that festered into hatred, Esau betrayed his own brother when foreigners attacked the nation of Israel. Instead of coming to the defense of his brother he cheered the enemy on and participated in the slaughter of his own flesh and blood. In fact, those who escaped were hunted down by Esau and handed over to the enemy (see the one-chapter book of Obadiah in the Bible).

For favor

Another reason people will betray others is for illicit favors from high places. David and his men had just engaged and defeated the enemy who had invaded Keilah, a city in Israel. Although he had risked his life and the lives of his men to rescue this city, he did not take it for granted that they will protect him from Saul.

> "When David learned that Saul was plotting against him, he said to Abiathar the priest, "Bring the ephod." [10] David said, "Lord, God of Israel, your servant has heard definitely that Saul plans to come to Keilah and destroy the town on account of me" (1 Samuel 23:9-10).

Why would people he had just fought to defend turn him over to the one seeking his life? Because they wanted to be in good standing with Saul in order to gain his favors. In these last days, people will increasingly seek favors with the powers that be and would not hesitate betraying those who have shown them kindness and helped them when they were in need.

Having looked at why people will increasingly resort to betraying others, in the next chapter, I would like us to see how we can defeat this spirit of betrayal.

Chapter Fourteen

How to defeat the spirit of Judas Iscariot – 1

The scripture have not left us in the dark with respect to how we can survive the onslaught of this spirit of betrayal, ensuring that we are never its victim. We will look at several strategies revealed in the word of God.

Do not easily trust people

Humans are fallible! This seems to be trivial knowledge. However, some put their trust in humans to the extent that their entire world come crashing down at the slightest betrayal. God does not place his trust in man, because He knows the human tendency to be unreliable. It is written that, "If God places no trust in his servants, if he charges his angels with error, [19] how much more those who live in houses of clay, whose foundations are in the dust, who are crushed more readily than a moth!" (Job 4:18-19). So, he commands you and me to "stop trusting in mere humans, who have but a breath in their nostrils. Why hold them in esteem?" (Isaiah 2:22).

That is a command many people are willing to obey only after they have become victims. In this regard to not easily trust people, the Bible applies it to every sphere of human relationships. He addresses community relationships (neighbor), friendships, family relationships, and matrimonial relationships. Listen to what the Lord says by the mouth of another prophet:

> "Do not trust a neighbor; put no confidence in a friend. Even with the woman who lies in your embrace guard the words of your lips. ^{6} For a son dishonors his father, a daughter rises up against her mother, a daughter-in-law against her mother-in-law— a man's enemies are the members of his own household" (Micah 7:5-6).

Let God validate your relationships

Whether it comes to a life partner, a friendship, a business partnership etc. it is always good to have the Lord who sees the end from the beginning validate it. Pray seriously about any relationship and listen to the voice of the Spirit before committing yourself to it. If you do this, you give the Spirit time to raise red flags where necessary. If we return to our story about David in Keilah, you see that David placed no trust in the people of the city even though he had just rescued them from an invading force. Take a read:

> "When David learned that Saul was plotting against him, he said to Abiathar the priest, "Bring the ephod." ^{10} David said, "Lord, God of Israel, your servant has heard definitely that Saul plans to come to Keilah and destroy the town on account of me. ^{11} Will the citizens of Keilah surrender me to him? Will Saul come down, as your servant has heard? Lord, God of Israel, tell your servant."

And the Lord said, "He will."

¹² Again David asked, "Will the citizens of Keilah surrender me and my men to Saul?"

And the Lord said, "They will."

¹³ So David and his men, about six hundred in number, left Keilah and kept moving from place to place. When Saul was told that David had escaped from Keilah, he did not go there." (1 Samuel 23:9-13).

Because David asked the Lord, the response from God made him escape with his life. Had he blindly trusted the people, he would have been a victim of his own negligence. There are so many people who have become victims of such negligence and later became angry with the Lord. In another instance when people came to support him access the throne while he was hiding from Saul, he did not quickly incorporate them until a word of prophecy came. In this case, the outcome was positive. He could let them fight alongside him without fear of being betrayed into the hands of those who sought to eliminate him.

"¹⁶ Other Benjamites and some men from Judah also came to David in his stronghold. ¹⁷ David went out to meet them and said to them, "If you have come to me in peace to help me, I am ready for you to join me. But if you have come to betray me to my enemies when my hands are free from violence, may the God of our ancestors see it and judge you."

¹⁸ Then the Spirit came on Amasai, chief of the Thirty, and he said:

"We are yours, David! We are with you, son of Jesse! Success, success to you, and success to those who help you, for your God will help you." So David received them and made them leaders of his raiding bands" (1 Chronicles 12:16-18)

Many times, people seem to trust the wrong people and suspect the right ones. Only the Lord's validation can take away every doubt and guarantee safety. I do not mean that anyone the Lord permits to be incorporated into your inner circle cannot turn against you one day. Judas too, like the other apostles, was chosen after much prayer by our Lord. His betraying the Lord helped fulfilled the Father's purpose for the Son and for mankind. This means when you have prayed and sought the Lord about your relationships and associations, any outcome thereafter will be in the will of the Father.

Avoid people who talk too much (gossip, slander)

There are people wo have not mastered the discipline of reining in their tongue. They can speak without any control from one topic to another and without even intending to or realizing it, they have divulged confidential information. Here is what the Bible says you should do:

"A gossip betrays a confidence, but a trustworthy person keeps a secret" (Proverbs 11:3)

"A gossip betrays a confidence; so avoid anyone who talks too much" (Proverbs 20:19).

Beware of and avoid those who don't visibly react to hurts (Learn to read the signs).

People who do not easily show a reaction when they are hurt, whether positive or negative tend to harbor grudges and will often seek revenge. A good example of this is seen in the case of Amnon, Tamar, and Absalom. Amnon had raped his half-sister who was the younger sister of Absalom.

> "Her brother Absalom said to her, "Has that Amnon, your brother, been with you? Be quiet for now, my sister; he is your brother. Don't take this thing to heart." And Tamar lived in her brother Absalom's house, a desolate woman.
>
> 21 When King David heard all this, he was furious. 22 And Absalom never said a word to Amnon, either good or bad; he hated Amnon because he had disgraced his sister Tamar" (1 Samuel 13:20-22).

Do you see the two contrasting reactions: David was furious, but Absalom showed no reaction. People who react will often cool down from their anger. Those who do not react still have their anger building up like a volcano.

King David and Amnon did not read the signs. They must have known how Absalom has reacted to other issues and deduced that this was an unusual nonreaction. Two years later he carried out his revenge and murdered Amnon (see 2 Samuel 13:23-28).

Beware of and avoid those who love money

Lovers of money are prone to betray others to satisfy their never satiating cravings for more money. Judas betrayed his Lord for money. Delilah betrayed her lover for money. We are seeing spouses betraying one another for money. To survive this spirit of betrayal you will need to avoid dealing at any very intimate personal level with those who have shown a propensity for the love of money.

In the case of Delilah in Judges 16:4-5, she was promised a huge some of money equivalent in today's measurements to about 13 Kgs of silver per ruler. Multiplied by the five rulers, that is about $41,000 at today's price for silver. If you factor in inflation and other parameters, it would be like hundreds of thousands of worth of today's dollar. Judas did not have that much offer, but he still betrayed his mater anyways for about three thousand dollars maximum.

Chapter Fifteen

How to defeat the spirit of Judas Iscariot – 2

In the last chapter we discussed some strategies to help us survive the onslaught of the spirit of betrayal. In this chapter, we will continue looking at further strategies to defeat this spirit.

Set boundaries around you

It is very important to set boundaries around yourself and have people respect those boundaries. You cannot afford to be openly accessible to everyone. While physical access is part of what I am discussing here, this goes far beyond physical access into emotional, mental, and even spiritual access. You can be accessible while not being openly accessible. Setting boundaries around you doesn't mean living behind a wall, it simply means erecting sentinels and alarm systems that call your attention to the ill-intentioned. Several times Paul exhorted the saints to be on their guard. The Lord himself asked his disciples to be on their guard.

There was a king in the Bible who failed to set boundaries or install personal sentinels around his physical environment. His name was Ish-Bosheth, the son of King Saul, and it cost him his life.

> "Now Rekab and Baanah, the sons of Rimmon the Beerothite, set out for the house of Ish-Bosheth, and they arrived there in the heat of the day while he was taking his noonday rest. [6] They went into the inner part of the house as if to get some wheat, and they stabbed him in the stomach. Then Rekab and his brother Baanah slipped away. [7] They had gone into the house while he was lying on the bed in his bedroom. After they stabbed and killed him, they cut off his head. Taking it with them, they traveled all night by way of the Arabah. [8] They brought the head of Ish-Bosheth to David at Hebron and said to the king, "Here is the head of Ish-Bosheth son of Saul, your enemy, who tried to kill you. This day the Lord has avenged my lord the king against Saul and his offspring." (2 Samuel 4:7-8).

These men were close collaborators of the king. Military leaders in his kingdom. They knew the routine of the king, where he would be and what he would be doing at what time of the day. They knew the security lapses around the king, and had easy access to the king. There were no sentinels, no alarm systems, no barriers around the king even when he was most vulnerable, sleeping. Not only did they have unchecked access to his inner chamber, they knew his storeroom and the different doors and connecting points. Note that they went into the inner part as if to get grain, so they were going into his storeroom. Probably he was so generous that any of his officials in need could come and get what they wanted.

Even after they killed and decapitated the king, no one was around to notice it. They mastered their way in and out of the palace.

You have to be careful of who you grant access into your very privacy. Everyone who has been betrayed was a victim of an insider who knew their routines. Set boundaries, set sentinels and alarm systems around you.

Keep away the power hungry

People who are hungry for power, position, or promotion are very susceptible to become vehicles of betrayal. We saw the case of Doeg the Edomite, who grew powerful by betraying others. To drive home this point, I would like us to consider another instance of a betrayer in quest for power.

King Saul had a servant called Ziba who was in charge of the king's property and managed his estate. When the king and his sons passed away on the war front, and after the death of the heir to the throne Ish-Bosheth, Mephibosheth was now heir to everything. The only problem is that he was young and crippled. Ziba saw his opportunity to become rich. Instead of being faithful to his duty and loyal to his master, he decided to betray even the dead and began using the estate as his personal property.

He made Mephibosheth to go and hid in Lodebar, a place of no pasture. I want to conjecture that he said to him, "David must not know that you are alive or you will lose your life". In fear, the heir to the estate of the former king lived in hiding and in poverty while Ziba profited from the estate. When David decided to show kindness to any descendant of his covenant friend, the late Jonathan, he was made to know of the existence of Ziba who was a servant of king Saul.

> "Then the king summoned Ziba, Saul's steward, and said to him, "I have given your master's grandson everything that belonged to Saul and his family. [10] You and your sons and your servants are to farm the land for him and bring in the crops, so that your master's grandson may be provided for. And Mephibosheth, grandson of your master, will always eat at my table." (Now Ziba had fifteen sons and twenty servants.)" (2 Samuel 9:9-10)

You see, Ziba had grown so rich that he had twenty servants. Now his sons were going to join his servants to work for Mephibosheth. I am sure he was not pleased with this in any way, so he watched for his opportunity. When Absalom rose up in rebellion against his own father, David had to flee. This power hungry traitor called Ziba decided that he would betray his master Mephibosheth. Instead of helping him escape, he ran and left him behind and went and slandered his master to David. These two passages below gives you a clearer picture of what happened:

> "When David had gone a short distance beyond the summit, there was Ziba, the steward of Mephibosheth, waiting to meet him. He had a string of donkeys saddled and loaded with two hundred loaves of bread, a hundred cakes of raisins, a hundred cakes of figs and a skin of wine. [2] The king asked Ziba, "Why have you brought these?"
>
> Ziba answered, "The donkeys are for the king's household to ride on, the bread and fruit are for the men to eat, and the wine is to refresh those who become exhausted in the

wilderness."³ The king then asked, "Where is your master's grandson?" Ziba said to him, "He is staying in Jerusalem, because he thinks, 'Today the Israelites will restore to me my grandfather's kingdom.'"⁴ Then the king said to Ziba, "All that belonged to Mephibosheth is now yours." "I humbly bow," Ziba said. "May I find favor in your eyes, my lord the king" (2 Samuel 16:1-4).

"24 Mephibosheth, Saul's grandson, also went down to meet the king. He had not taken care of his feet or trimmed his mustache or washed his clothes from the day the king left until the day he returned safely. 25 When he came from Jerusalem to meet the king, the king asked him, "Why didn't you go with me, Mephibosheth?" 26 He said, "My lord the king, since I your servant am lame, I said, 'I will have my donkey saddled and will ride on it, so I can go with the king.' But Ziba my servant betrayed me. 27 And he has slandered your servant to my lord the king. My lord the king is like an angel of God; so do whatever you wish. 28 All my grandfather's descendants deserved nothing but death from my lord the king, but you gave your servant a place among those who eat at your table. So what right do I have to make any more appeals to the king?" 29 The king said to him, "Why say more? I order you and Ziba to divide the land." 30 Mephibosheth said to the king, "Let him take everything, now that my lord the king has returned home safely." (2 Samuel 19:24-30)

Ziba was a master at manipulation. He was not interested in David. His actions were well calculated to turn David against Mephibosheth so that he, Ziba could return to using the proceeds of the land for himself and his family. If he was indeed working the land for his master, how come he took all those supplies to David without his master's permission? Either he was lying, or he was being disloyal to his master. Beware of people who constantly complain to you about others or try to turn you against others.

Beware of those who flatter you

It is the human tendency to become vulnerable to those who sing one's praise. Flattery is a weapon that the enemy has used over time to gain access into circles and lives of people. If you have a heart that delights in human praise you become an easy prey. People who never confront you with the truth are more dangerous than those who may even criticize you. These verses from scripture written thousands of years ago paint a true picture of today's society:

> "Help, Lord, for no one is faithful anymore; those who are loyal have vanished from the human race. ² Everyone lies to their neighbor; they flatter with their lips but harbor deception in their hearts" (Psalm 12:1-2).

> "Your relatives, members of your own family—even they have betrayed you; they have raised a loud cry against you. Do not trust them, though they speak well of you". (Jerimiah 12:6)

> "Their tongue is a deadly arrow; it speaks deceitfully. With their mouths they all speak cordially to their neighbors, but in their hearts they set traps for them" (Jerimiah 9:8)

It is highly probable that those who flatter you are trying to coverup something they are extracting from you or are purposely setting you up for a great self-fall. The masters of deception; the Pharisees and

Sadducees employed the same strategy of flattery in order to set the Lord Jesus up:

> "Keeping a close watch on him, they sent spies, who pretended to be sincere. They hoped to catch Jesus in something he said, so that they might hand him over to the power and authority of the governor. [21] So the spies questioned him: "Teacher, we know that you speak and teach what is right, and that you do not show partiality but teach the way of God in accordance with the truth. [22] Is it right for us to pay taxes to Caesar or not?" [23] He saw through their duplicity and said to them, [24] "Show me a denarius. Whose image and inscription are on it?" Caesar's," they replied. [25] He said to them, "Then give back to Caesar what is Caesar's, and to God what is God's."
>
> [26] They were unable to trap him in what he had said there in public. And astonished by his answer, they became silent "(Luke 20:20-26).

The Lord saw through their duplicity because he listened beyond the words that were being uttered. Many people would have fallen into this simple plan and ended their ministry before time. Do not be easily carried away by the praise of men.

Beware of people with a sense of entitlement and those who show ingratitude

People with a sense of entitlement have a tendency to seek the easy way out. They will readily embrace any shortcut to power, position, or possessions even if it means betraying someone else's trust. King Saul thought he was entitled to the throne of Israel, and that his descendants were also entitled to the throne of Israel. Consequently, he was willing to betray David's loyalty and dedication to the kingdom and people of Israel. He was ready to betray his own son and daughter, and son in-law to cling to power even though he had been rejected by God.

Jonathan was not like his father. He did not have a sense of entitlement and so he protected David from being killed. Had he a sense of entitlement he would have betrayed his covenant friendship with David in order to inherit the throne of his father Saul. On the other hand, Absalom, had a sense of entitlement to the throne and was ready to kill his own father so that he could ascend the throne even before it was his turn.

Another example of an ungrateful person who felt entitled and betrayed his family is Abimelek. He conspired with people from his mother's clan and murdered seventy of his own father's children because he wanted to be ruler (see Judges 9). King Solomon also killed his own brother because he felt offended that he asked for Abishag, which Solomon felt he was entitled to marry after becoming king. A sense of entitlement is an indicator of a heart inclined to betray.

Beware of people who want to have every information about you

Some people come around you just to gather information on behalf of those who've made themselves your enemies. Usually, these people hate you just because of what you are doing for the Lord or what you have accomplished and become in life in spite of their opposition or secret wishes otherwise. Or maybe they just feel threatened by you for no reason. Such individuals will ask information about your life, marriage, ministry, business etc. to which they have no right to know. I call such people ziphites. To understand more about the ziphites see 1 Samuel 23:19-23.

Be like the wind

One great prophet of blessed memory used to say, "what people do not understand, they criticize; what they understand, they destroy". That is why as a believer you cannot afford to be predictable. Not everyone should know what button in your life to press to obtain what outcome. The easier you are to understand, the easier you are to manipulate. Think of it, anyone can manipulate a bicycle because it is very easy to understand. Likewise, a car. The more complicated it becomes the fewer the people who can manipulate it. Fewer are the people who can manipulate trains, fewer still can manipulate airplanes, and very few can manipulate space shuttles.

The Lord Jesus said,

"⁸ The wind blows wherever it pleases. You hear its sound, but you cannot tell where it comes from or where it is going. So it is with everyone born of the Spirit" (John 3:8).

To defeat the spirit of betrayal, you will have to become like the wind. Let it be difficult for people to predict you. If they cannot predict you, they cannot program you, and if they cannot program you, it will be difficult for them to betray you.

Having looked at how to defeat this spirit of Judas Iscariot, in the next chapter, we will explain how one can be delivered from this spirit.

Chapter Sixteen

Deliverance from the spirit of betrayal

The spirit of betrayal is one of those things that every human being is susceptible to if one doesn't consciously guard against. What I mean is, every human being has the potential to become a traitor depending on who is concerned. Why is it so? Because we all have the potential to be selfishly ambitious. However, given the opportunity to betray, some will fall for it while others will deliberately shun it. It is a good thing when one is conscious of this negative potential in every human being to betray. This consciousness makes you guard against this spirit, first of all in your life, and secondly in those around you.

Like with every other bondage to evil spirits or characters, there are simple effective steps to follow so as to gain total freedom. Follow these steps and receive your freedom. Again, since you do not really know your own heart, pray all the way.

1. Plead the blood of Jesus on yourself spirit, soul, and body, family, property, job/ business/ ministry, finances etc.
2. Thank the Lord for His victory over the works of satan

3. Thank the Lord for His power available to set free captives
4. Ask the Lord to forgive you for anyway you have allowed the spirit of Judas Iscariot to operate in your life. it is advisable to pray through the list:
   - Love of money
   - Love of power,
   - Love of position
   - Love of possession
   - Jealousy
   - Hatred
   - Discontentment
   - Disloyalty
   - Love of ease and shortcuts
   - Gossip
   - slander
   - Talkativeness
   - Being too inquisitive
   - Selfish ambition
5. Renounce these manifestations listed above and separate your heart from each.
6. Declare the victory of the cross over satan and his cohorts, and break every grip of the spirit of betrayal over your life.
7. Now, by faith, bind and cast out the spirit of Judas Iscariot from your life.

8. Proclaim your freedom from the spirit of Judas Iscariot and thank the Lord for His victory in your life
9. Close every door in your life to this spirit and seal it with the blood of Jesus.

Conclusion

In this volume, we have examined four different end time spirits, the way you can recognize them, how to can defeat them, and how you can obtain personal deliverance from such spirits. You may need to go through it a second, and a third time to really grasp and effectively implement the strategies shared in this book. In the next volume of the series, we will take a detailed look into other end time spirits and equip ourselves on how to effectively deal with them and live as victors, and not victims, in these end times.

For questions and counselling write to

Dr. Celestine Nakeli

Karlstraße 4

75053 Gondelsheim

Germany

www.ingramcontent.com/pod-product-compliance
Lightning Source LLC
Chambersburg PA
CBHW061801070526
44586CB00023B/2663